Dedicated to me,
Because I owe this to myself

To my big sister *Jadyn,*
For getting me out of my comfort zone
And being my biggest supporter

And my twin flame *Jayda Cordes,*
For having the biggest heart
and holding me up through all of this

What am I going to do with you, my love?

We can't keep this much longer

Your life is about to begin,

And mine still at a halt from the from the day you broke my heart

You'll forget all about me,

And I'll still be here writing your name in the dedication

Maybe i'm the joker in your deck of cards,
Useful for some games,
But not counted in the total number of cards.
So am I worth keeping in the deck?
Or do you throw me away

A house of cards never stands for very long

I wish I could apologize to everyone i've ever met
Don't try to give me your forgiveness
Just let me apologize for every mistake i've made
For not calling when I should've,
For not telling you that I love you more often,
For taking up any of your thoughts,
Let me apologize and then let me go
Let me float into the stars so that I should never have to
apologize again

It's funny how people are so easily influenced by anything.

It's funny how you can stop eating when things go south.

Or how you do something impulsive one time
And suddenly you have stars drawn around your scars.

How funny this cycle becomes a pattern known all too well.

There is a delicacy between two people who come together
for a brief moment,
Two people who have bared their souls to each other in the
past,
Come together on a level of understanding.
You both promised to always be there,
And the promise still stands in these moments.

On New Years i'll make a resolution to get over you

On Valentine's day i'll be reminded of you

On my birthday i'll blow out candles wishing I could forget about you

On summer nights i'll ask the moon why I still think about you

On Thanksgiving i'll be grateful for you

On Christmas I only want you back

I'm out of fight.
My brian and body are disconnected.
I'm missing the important moments of life.
Yell at me
Scream at me
You will get nothing in return.
Like talking to a brick wall.
My will to live is weak,
Like my inability to stand.
No thoughts behind my eyes.
Not even observing the things around me.
Just kind of here
Taking up space.
Like a picture on a wall
Put up for others' amusement.

Your body has its own way of telling you you're not healed.
When your brain has you fully convinced that you've moved on.
It's heartbreaking when you realize that all this time you've been healing,
You didn't even consider the broken bones and bruises begging for help.
You're left in the dark,
With no idea how to fix what's broken.
You put a cast on a broken bone in order for it to heal properly,
But you can't force it to be fixed.
You can only give it time.

I may not be the kind of girl you marry,
Or even the girl you take home to your parents.
But I would hope I'm the girl that gave you enough happy
memories to fill your thoughts once in a while.
I hope I'm not as easily forgettable as I am easy to leave.

I don't believe in holding grudges,
They tear us apart
Putting our mind and souls at war

Our soul wanting to forgive and be free,
Our mind fighting for its own peace

People make mistakes

That's what they say right?

Majority of the time, Beautiful things don't last for very long.

It's unfortunate, because once you've experienced something beautiful, you'll wish you could see it just one more time once it's gone. You'll wish you took your time admiring it the first time.

You might even start comparing its beauty to something else,

Trying to relive the feeling you had.

You can try and try again, but it will never be the same.

You have to walk away knowing you only got to experience it one time.

Understand that in a world full of billions, you got to experience this beautiful thing.

You got to *live* it, to *feel* it.

Don't worry, you will find your next beautiful thing.

At the right place,

At the right time,

You'll see it.

Hold on to it tight, they don't stay for very long.

I'm here
In this room again
This room that encloses my mind.
The lights are off
Nothing but the sound of my quivering breath.
Shivering from the cold,
Or the intrusive thoughts.
The walls move in,
As they always do.
I don't fight.
I don't push them back.
Instead they enclose my last breath.
My moment of peace has come for me,
It takes me in its grasp,
Like a warm hug.
The shivers stop.
The thoughts stop.
I am home.

You don't swarm my thoughts like you used to anymore.
But sometimes I imagine you in my passenger seat,
Blasting our songs like we used to.
Or sometimes I'll see a car like yours,
And I take my eyes off the road to see that it's not you.
I still wonder if you're doing okay.
I imagine you getting out of this town and being happy.
Maybe we'll bump into each other in the future,
And maybe we'll catch up.
But that's all just in my head.
I tend to see the best version of you up there.

My mom has no respect for you anymore.
My sisters telling me that I have no self respect for letting
this happen
Over and over again.
Everyone tells me to go,
But we both know I'll never be the one to leave.

"What are you so afraid of?"

Becoming you.

I think I'm stronger than I really am.

I don't give it a second thought if I'm questioning whether or not I can handle something.

Of course I can handle it.

I will figure it out

I always do.

Life doesn't stop for anyone.

People come and go.

I've been reshaping myself to fit the needs of everyone around me for as long as I can remember.

I don't know any better.

Maybe letting people hurt me is my love language.

At least they wanted *something* from me.

I see right through you.
I have since the first time you looked at me.
The thick wall you put up for everyone,
Becomes transparent to me.
I think you're aware of it happening,
So you avoid my eyes.
But I still see you.
Why do you still try to hide after all this time?

You have to live in your body so why drain yourself picking it apart?
Build it up instead.
Go to the gym until you're on a first name basis with the employees.
The soreness becomes your trophy.
You're addicted.
Push yourself even harder than you have been everyday.
Keep going.
No one will do it for you.
Be someone you look up to.
When you're out of fight,
Keep going.
You have to keep going.

I forgive to easily
I don't sleep much,
I still wait for you to call me.
I write to think,
I take medication to feel normal,
I stay in contact with the people who've hurt me.
I process pain by running away,
Until it finds me at my happiest moments.
In some deranged way,
I hope you'll still be around,
To tell me I'm not easy to forget.
I love people on a scale of how bad they've hurt me.
I never know when to let go.
I know everything and nothing about myself.

I know that everything around me is art.
I know that everything deserves to be appreciated.
I try my best to see only the beauty in things.
Even the things that are not beautiful at all,
Like the scars on my arms,
Or the visions of you taking my body like it was yours to
begin with.
These things live inside me,
Infecting everything it touches.
Yet I still dust it off and be gentle with it,
Until it becomes something people admire in a museum.

I don't hear from you all day or all night.

But honey you're still in my dreams all night.

There's something poetic about piggybacks.

Being so close to someone

Giving your trust in them to hold you up

A new eyeline to see the things you might have missed

Even if I fall

I'll fall with you.

The room is too bright.

There's too many conversations.

My socks don't sit right, and my shoes are too loose.

The letters are moving,

What do the words say?

I can't understand you,

I don't know what's going on.

Are you talking to me?

What are you saying?

The rings on my fingers are making my hands sweat. I can't get them off.

My head hurts,

My vision is blurry,

There's too much noise.

My head is hot, and full of thoughts.

Too many to know what they're saying.

I have too much to do,

I can't get it done.

I can't focus.

It's all too much.

My eyes are tearing, my body numb.

My brain is shutting down,

And I'm gone.

I feel as though I am only bearable in small doses.
If I linger too long I become insufferable.
Even for my mind.

Go to sleep in the same jewelry you never change.
Wake up and put more on.

I love your bracelet

Keep it.
It's yours now.

I like that shirt on you

Have it.

Can I borrow a sweatshirt?

Of course.
Pick whatever you want.
Keep it, It looks better on you.

Are they just material things?
Or will they be reminders of me when I'm gone.

To be used is to dry out a marker and put it back in the box.

You suddenly changed your mind,

You only want crayons now.

With no explanation,

You watch them enjoy their new crayons.

They treat them with delicacy.

Using only the slightest pressure to ensure its shape.

Never running dry,

Never changing minds,

Pruned and left behind,

You hold out hope.

They'll need me again when they need a bold line to hold them.

Ambition lies in all of us. You can see it in everyone's eyes. From a newborn baby to a woman in her latest years. Everyone is constantly learning and evolving. We live and breathe in this universe everyday. When we become unsatisfied with our lives, we yearn for more. To find something in our lives we think we've lost. You look everywhere. Under the couch cushions and in the crevices of our trauma. But why do we search the house and pick apart our brains for an answer that was within us the whole time? Our bodies hold our truths for our entire existence. We are capable of handling every problem we are faced with. Our skeletons and skin protect all the questions, answers, experiences, and truths to be released as we grow old. Is that why our elders get stiff joints and sore backs? Because they no longer hold an answer their body was keeping from them? It's as simple as counting on yourself. Focus on what your body is telling you. Reflect on it. And you will know what to do.

No matter how much they hurt you,
Or how often you think about what they did,
There's a part of you that will always hold onto the love you
had.
That small part of you that won't let you forget.
Even though you have more reason to hate them,
This piece of you holds onto the love you felt.
As you watch them move on from a distance,
You wonder if a piece of their heart is saved for you.

I want to stop loving the people that hurt me.

I want to stop trying to understand their pain more than my own.

I don't want to forgive you for what you did to me.

I wish I could hate you as much as I love you.

There's a certain comfort in being sad.

A comfort in going back to your old ways.

They don't tell you this when you learn about the effects of depression.

I mean,

How could you not find comfort in a feeling you've only ever known?

It's the only thing that stays consistent in your life.

So you do it.

You let it sink back into your life,

Like an oil spill that never fully leaves the ocean.

You felt it coming.

And this time you don't fight it.

You welcome the overwhelming wave of sorrow and guilt as it covers you like a warm blanket.

You know you're going to be here awhile,

So you get comfortable.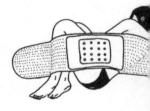

You don't leave your bed.

You don't even check your phone.

You just let it take over.

Turning your thoughts into nothingness,

And your body motionless.

You're almost grateful for this emptiness you feel.

Things that would normally bother you,

Just don't anymore.

You imagine the ocean waves taking you away as you sink further into the water.

I feel the guilt wash over me when I hope for something
good to come into my life.
Do I deserve it?
Probably not.
But just this once,
I don't want to have to learn from something.

I told you i'd wait forever for you to be ready
And I meant it
I would wait forever and always to be with you

But life doesn't give up forever and always does it?
Because things with us are different
We don't say anything about it,
We just kiss and move on

I asked you to be mine
So you know how much I love you
You told me you needed time
So I'll know how much you love me

If i'm going to wait forever and always for you
Will you just please respond to my one text
Will you please just tell me that my clothes are still on your
pillow not in your closet

Please just give me something to know that you're still there

Music is my love language.
I love the way a song can effortlessly say the thing I could
never say out loud.
Telling you the things I'm too afraid to say.

The day you decided our song meant nothing more to you,
Was the day that I set you free.

Are you happy with the way things ended?
Are you content knowing you broke the girl that would've
done anything to see your smile?
I don't know how you do it.
Why did *you* get the handbook on how to move on,
And I didn't even know that book existed.

I'm always waiting for something,
I can't quite put my finger on what it is i'm waiting for,
When conflicts arrive in my life it's easy to shrug off
Because I'm already waiting for something worse,
And they do,
Worse and worse things appear,
Just as I had expected,
And I keep waiting for more.

Everyone says that heartbreak is your opportunity to find
yourself,
To dig deep and heal those inner wounds,
So that you may feel happy in your own skin.

What If there's nothing to heal?
What if I fully healed my wounds when I was with her?
How do I go back to that time of bliss,
When I had no more inner wounds because of her?

You don't have to live your life waiting for people to love you

You can live your life falling in love with new things everyday.

All the things in my head,
A spiral of words and destruction,
I find their sweet spot,
And I translate them into the simplest form,
Spilling these pages with bad poetry

Others may call it seasonal depression and anticipate our comeback.

They push us to live because we can no longer push ourselves.

Days and months go by,

People get bored and move on.

You fill your pillows with tears,

And your journals with spiraling thoughts,

Reflecting on your once full life,

Looking to the stars for answers,

Trying to remember where your ambition went.

You don't want any help,

You don't want anyone to know.

You finally get yourself out of the bed you've laid in for months,

Life didn't stop for you.

You can't help but feel the irreplaceable damage you've done.

The same damage you will pass onto your children.

The few good times don't outweigh the bad

Read that again

Weather it was intentional or not,
Someone did this to me.
I'm angry,
I want to scream from the rooftops,
Scream to the universe that I didn't deserve this.
Maybe if I beg and plead,
Nothing like this will ever happen again.
But it will.
Over and over again.
This will be with me for the rest of my life.
Irreversible damage has been done.

Maybe i'm angry because I can't blame this on myself,
It would be so much easier if this resulted from my own
actions,
I've picked it apart from every angle,
Trying to find a way I can take the blame.
But I've found nothing.
Why would I want to take the blame for something
someone did to me?
Why would I want to be in the wrong?
So it could be easier to heal and move on?
So I might learn something from it?
The only thing I've learned from this,
Is that I'm disposable
And someone took advantage of that.

You're not a constant self improvement project

You say you love me,
But treat me like you've already lost me.

Why couldn't you listen to me when I told you something
was wrong?
You don't believe me unless it's written out and signed by a
therapist.

You take my love when you need it,
And disappear when I need you.

It was my mistake for thinking you loved me enough to tell me the truth.

Often I feel like a freshly fallen leaf.
Manipulated to go wherever the wind takes me.
Purposely stepped on and raked away.
I wonder if my suffering is a game for you.
You lay down a field of promises and then blow them away.
You make sure to stay in my life long enough so that you can
rake me up and throw me away whenever you please.
I laid down everything I had for you to walk over.
You had me fooled into thinking fall was your favorite
season.
If this is all a game for you,
Then you don't play fairly.
It was my mistake for ignoring the warning signs,
Just so I could have you.

I'll still come back every fall so you can rake me up all over
again.

I don't want to forgive people just so they'll stay in my life.

I don't want to accept your apologies only so you'd stop yelling.

I don't want to take the blame simply because you can't take responsibility.

I don't want to act unaffected because your feelings are more important than mine.

I don't want to live in a hole anymore.

Was it all a dream?
Did I imagine all of it?
It was over before it even started.
You didn't even give me a chance.
I just wanted to be enough for you.
I wanted to make you happy.
I don't know where I went wrong.
I really did try.
I'm sorry to see that you're happier without me.

If these walls could talk they'd say,
You're too young to be holding this much

I would say,
But you do it everyday

If this bed could talk it would say,
You can't let this hold you back, go see the world

And I would say,
But you hold me with such comfort

If these walls could talk,
Would I listen?

The promises you made,
In your bed I laid
All the sweet lies,
And I still stayed.

I'll need first aid,
But you ran away.

In my mind you're still mine
But in your eyes I find,
Your heart is no longer mine.

Yes, I'll admit, I am very easily manipulated.

In my mind I think of it as giving people the benefit of the doubt.

Refusing to see anything but the good in people.

But people like you only see that as easily manipulated.

You use it to your advantage.

To see just how much you can get away with,

Without me even realizing what's happening.

You know i'll forgive you anyway,

So what's the harm right?

I chip away parts of myself in order to connect with
everyone I meet,
Like one big puzzle.
But when you start resenting me for how you asked me to
be,
I'm left in the dark,
With nothing of myself left,
I'll scramble to find what you want from me this time.
Questioning why I wasn't enough.
I did what you wanted,
And it still wasn't enough.
A puzzle can never be finished with missing pieces.

The way you hurt me
Cannot be put into words

You tether my heart like a puppet,
Putting on a show for anyone to see.
No one knows what you did to me.
Not a soul knows why I keep letting you.

I don't know what our relationship is anymore.
It feels like a rocky bridge hanging over an angry river.
We're both standing in the middle,
Waiting for the bridge to collapse.
Sending us down the river,
Ripping us in different directions.
We stay on the bridge,
Knowing what could happen,
But neither of us are scared.
Neither of us move.
We just wait.

I'm trying to listen to what you're saying,
But I'm looking down at my own body.
The only thing I can do is look up,
Trying to pull myself out of the stars and back into reality.
When I finally have something to say
You give up and put the car in drive.

It's not something I talk about anymore.
Because if I don't talk about it,
Then no one will know I'm still doing it.
The same patterns I've shaped my life around.

But it's becoming noticeable.
I can't turn it off.
How much longer do I have to keep doing this.

The answers are all around me,
But I look away everytime,
Even when they come straight for me,
I still duck,
I don't want to hurt anymore,
But I don't want this to be the end of us.

It was *you* who wanted me.
Do you remember that?
You were chasing *me*.
What happened to make you leave so fast?
Before I could even blink,
You were gone.

All around me
People are begging me to speak
Speak up about what I want
What I'm feeling
But I have nothing to say
I just sit here and absorb your words
My brain can't even put sentences together for a response
I was never good at scrabble.

I'm still looking to the 8ball for an answer

And finally

The outlook is good

You called me by the name you gave me
What was once music to my ears,
Is now a siren song

To the forgivers,

To the people who sympathize with the ones that have hurt them.
To the people who will always defend that one person.

To the dreamers,

To the people who spend their time trying to heal what wasn't broken.
The people who've embraced the idea of giving more than they'll ever receive.

To the people who spend so much time in their thoughts,
They begin to understand the phrase,
"Alone but not lonely"

These people whom I love dearly,
Are the people who've had their hearts broken too many times,
It's beyond repair.

These are the people who connect the stars with their words,
Hoping you'll read it in the same sky.

Moving on is not a simple act,
It's not a perfect straight line,
It's an endless loop of twists and turns,
Everyday comes with its ups and downs,
It overwhelms your everyday life,
Everything reminds you of them,
You can't even have a simple thought without being
reminded of them,
How easily they left you,
How they don't have a clue how hurt you are

My love,
I know how bad you're hurting,
I know that even the people around you can't make you feel
less isolated,
I know you're stuck in different feelings,
It's overwhelming and scary and not what you deserve,
You have so much love to give,
I'm sorry someone tried to take it from you

Sometimes my bracelets move down my arms and expose my truth.

The dull pattern and lines are uncovered for the world to see.

I can't help but stare like everybody else in the room.

I wonder how they got there,

Unable to imagine myself doing that.

What story does each one hold?

Was it worth it if I can't even remember?

Tell me about the way you hurt,
Show me the things you hold in your heart,
Take my hand and give it all to me,
Let me life it from your shoulders,
I can't bear to see you in pain,
Let me take it all,
Let me bandage you with the wrap of my embrace

I think you were always meant to know me a little better
than anyone else.
Our lives becoming a cosmic dance.
A terrible distance between us.
Our bodies are made of stardust,
And we are traveling through space towards the most
beautiful collision.

If the day should come,
And my body chips away,
I'm afraid there will be nothing but a shadow left.

You   Always   Have   And
   Always   Will   Be

My Muse

All the tears I shed,

And the hate I had for loving you still,

Would all be blown away,

The moment you realize,

That my embrace would be enough to take your sorrows

away.

Baby if it's puppy love,
You're the only one I can love like this

My love you are all the rom coms used to watch on repeat,
Waiting and wondering when it was going to be my turn

Couldn't bear to look at you,
I'd never look away

You put me in a trance,
Every minute of my day altared for you

Wake up earlier and earlier to see you,
Waste pointless time to wait for your response,
Loose hours of sleep to write you letters,
Go back and read old texts to miss you more

This isn't puppy love,
I've fallen in love with you,
My new home in your arms,
My new life in your eyes

For so long I thought i'd lost the best thing that had ever happened to me,
And I blamed myself for what happened,
But finally I realize that I never deserved what you did,
I will never let someone do that to me again,
Thank you for opening my eyes when I would've been content on keeping them shut.

No you can't have my peace anymore.
I'm sorry I let you have control of it for so long.
Suddenly you look at me with nothing but hatred in your
eyes.
I used to think it was you and me against the world.
But there's only so much I can take.
There's only so many times I can listen to you tell me you
wish I didn't exist.
I'm tired.
I've given all I have.
This is where it ends with us.

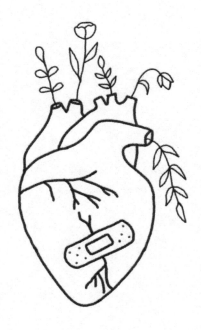

You still exist in my memories
So don't tell me it was hard to leave me
When I still see you behind my eyes

I'm not scared anymore,
Not of the dark,
And not of living.
All that time I wasted wishing my life away,
All the experiences I missed,
I don't want to miss anything anymore.
My life is mine only,
No matter how many people try to control it.

Funny how the flowers I bought for myself always lived longer than the ones you gave.

You put me in the donate box when you decided to move
on.

Cramped in this box with all the other meaningless things,
I became damaged
You didn't bother putting a **FRAGILE** sticker on.
My stitching came undone,
Leaving tears and bits of fabric to float through the closed
box.
You drive to the donation center and toss me in with no
hesitation.
You have to do what's best for you.
I was just taking up space anyway.
I pick up the broken pieces and stitch myself back together.
But the pieces don't fit right anymore.
Too much damage has been done.
Mangled together i'm thrown on the **MUST GO** rack,
Waiting for the next person who thinks they can fix me.

Sometimes I feel guilty for growing up.
I know it's stupid and growing up is one of the few things
everybody goes through.
I feel guilty because I know my parents preferred me when I
was a little.
I know i'll always be their little girl,
But it's different.
They loved me more when I didn't remind them of
themselves.

That was fun wasn't it?
I liked the part when you made me the happiest girl alive
That was the part when I promised myself I would never ask
for anything else,
Because I had you
I don't like this part
This is the part when I think about you everyday but I never
tell you
This is the part when you forget all about me

You asked me why I didn't tell you what was going on in my
head
Why would I?
You've given me countless reasons not to trust you
Why would I tell you something so delicate,
Just for you to run and tell everyone?

Somewhere along the way my reflection changed.
This person in the mirror doesn't look like me anymore.
It's haunting,
The way this reflection looks at me.

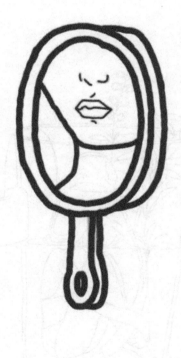

A girl's mind is an art that not even the disturbed wish to visit.
Overly emotional and distressed,
Admirable and thoughtful,
A girls mind is many things,
But it is not to be displayed.
No one really wants to know the truth behind her eyes.

I was born without a voice.
Unable to speak,
My thoughts become too big to hold.
I'll let you speak for me,
 For I'm scared of what will come out if I try.
I'll never tell you what i'm thinking,
But I will fill these pages with the words I cannot say.

I told you that Lilies of the Valley were my favorite flower.
You told me they were beautiful and asked me why they
were my favorite.
Because,
They'll break your heart with just one touch.

Lily of the Valley (Convallaria Majalis)
Has the flower meaning of sweetness, purity, happiness and
is said to bring luck in love.
The lily contains heart-active substances responsible for
cardiac arrhythmias and even death.

I feel the guilt wash over me when I hope for something
good to come in my life,
Do I deserve it?
Probably not
But just this once,
I don't want to have to learn from something.

Are you happy with the way things ended?
Are you content knowing you broke the girl that would've
done anything to see you smile?
I don't know how you do it.
Why did *you* get the handbook on how to move on,
And I didn't even know that book existed.

All this time has passed,
Yet I can't shake the nightmare of what you did,
It wakes me in my sleep,
Shaking in a cold sweat,
Visions of you laughing as I told you to stop,

In my room,
In the dark,
I'm scared of being in my own bed,
I can feel your ghost in it with me,
I can't ignore the fear that you'll do it again,

I won't be strong enough,
If this nightmare becomes real again,
I will break,
You will never see me again

You were always busy,
I admired your ambition,
You weren't afraid to take what you wanted,
I changed my schedule,
I rewrote my life to fit yours,
Hoping to just get a chance with you,
That was my biggest mistake.
Because when you left,
You took my whole life with you.

Everyone breaks down at some point

The kind of breakdown that feels like you're being stabbed
in the throat while trying to gasp for air

The breakdown that you think you won't come back from

Everything that's ever been wrong in your life plays in your
mind on an endless loop

It spreads throughout your body, gluing you to the floor

Nothing makes sense in this moment except for the angry
self-loathing thoughts

Maybe I was so deep under your spell that I imagined all of it

Maybe you didn't feel the same at all

Maybe I was lying to myself the whole time

If that's true then enjoy your oscar for best actress

Hypnotized by the dashed lines on the road in front of me,
I think about where this road could take me,
If I just drove,
Never looked back.
No one would notice if I left,
So why not keep going

By the end I was the only one fighting for us,
I had to convince myself that you still cared about me,
But I was delusional,
I knew things were different,
We went from talking everyday,
Living with a permanent smile on my face,
And constant butterflies in my stomach,
To putting my phone on dnd so I didn't have to see how
long you would choose to ignore me.
Your mood towards me changes dramatically,
Seeing me became a chore for you,
I should've known,
I should've said something,
I refused to believe I could lose you,
It was the most gut wrenching feeling I've ever known.

Why didn't you fight for me?

Why couldn't we have talked about it?

Why did you have to make this decision for the both of us?

I'm a person too, you know.

I would've done anything to fight for you to stay.

You knew you didn't see a future with me,

The least you could've done is tell me,

Instead of making promises you knew you'd break.

I wish I could give you a hug and tell you that everything's going to be alright

\-   Mirror mirror on the wall

You become the people you surround yourself with.
Whether you realize it or not, it's an act of nature.
You won't realize it until you do. You realize that you've
become a reflection of someone. You start talking like them,
liking the same things, and maybe even start to look like
them. You can't stop this from happening while continuing
the relationship. But you do have a choice of who you
reflect. If you choose to surround yourself with negative
energy, you will become that energy.

You can twist the story any way you want
You can find ways to make it my fault
You do whatever you have to do to make yourself feel better
But i'll always know
What really happened
And that story will die with me

You knew what you were doing

I don't want to share any part of myself with you anymore.

Note from the Author

You made it through! Thank you so much for reading this. I'm so grateful to have this opportunity. I never thought anyone would read these besides me. These pages are what got me through my worst times. I hope they gave you some clarity to whatever it is you might be going through. I hope that after reading this, you might try letting yourself be vulnerable. But most of all, I hope that no one has experienced the things I wrote about. No one deserves any of the pain I described. But if you do know what i'm talking about, and you have experienced this pain, don't hesitate to reach out for help. Tell people what is going on in your head.

Made in the USA
Monee, IL
13 November 2023

46391579R00059